This book is brought
to you by cats.
**"All facts have been collected
by cats and are true"**
*Milo, age 8
& a very good boy.*

Thank you for diving into this literary
rollercoaster! Once you're through, let me know
if you giggled, gasped, or spat out your tea.
A review on Amazon
would be really appreciated;
it's like giving this masterpiece a high-five!

For more of my work I'm on instagram

 @PeteRossDoodles

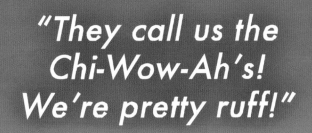

The average sausage dog
needs to consume
25 sausages a day to
maintain their form.

Dogs are secretly aliens from a planet made entirely of tennis balls.

Dalmatians sell their spots for tennis balls.

All dogs dream of being
**astronauts.**

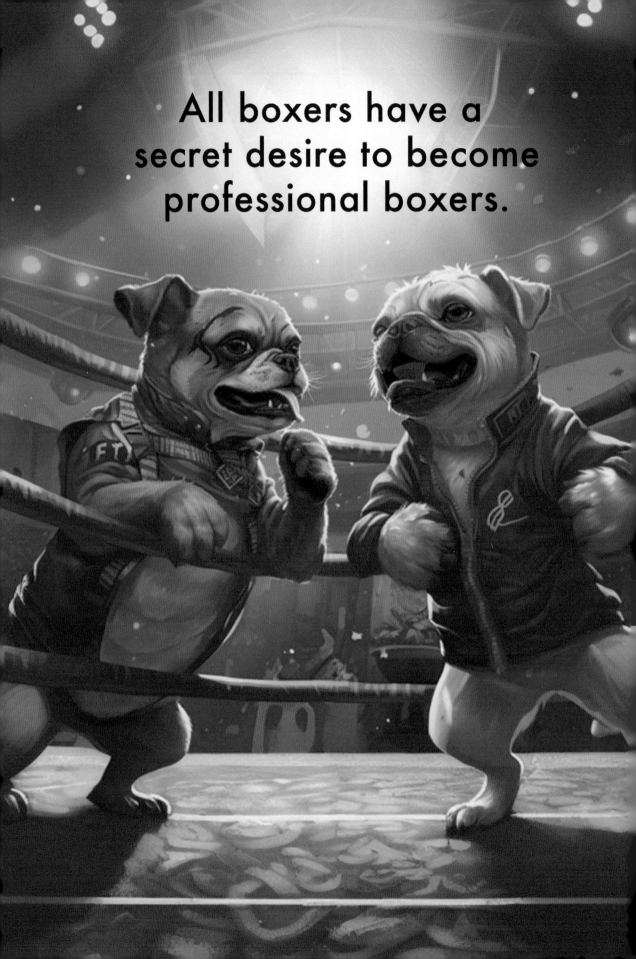

Poodles invented kung fu

Maltese dogs are from Malta
and made of Maltesers.

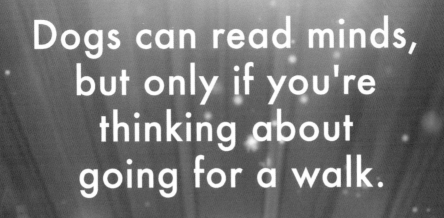

Dogs can read minds,
but only if you're
thinking about
going for a walk.

Bruce loves a wig

This is Rick.
He is the Michael Cera
of the dog world.

If you put a beret on a
French Bulldog
it explodes into 500 croissants.

All dogs are naturally musical,
they can play any instrument.

Mark Zuckerberg regularly transforms into a dog to listen to your conversations.

The 1995 film Waterworld correctly predicted the end of the world except it was dogs that survived not humans.

German Shepherds swoon over German shepherds!

When dogs roll around in the grass, they're actually practicing their ninja moves.

Every night, all dogs sneak out for a secret rave in a mystical forest with their best friends.

The world's smallest dog
is actually a
chihuahua named
Hercules.

Great Danes are actually small horses pretending to be dogs so they can come in the house.

When dogs howl at the moon, they're really just practicing their yodelling skills.

South Koreans
love a peekapoo.

The best breakdancers in
the world are poodles.

Shih Tzus
are named after
underperforming zoos.

Fans love dogs
and dogs love fans.

Pomeranians live on a diet of chaos.

Dogs are 99% wolf.

This is true.

Printed in Great Britain
by Amazon

33441172R00021